THE
MODIFIED
TOOLBOX

Presented by The Modified Gentleman

THE MODIFIED TOOLBOX

Transformative thoughts to expand your Focus,
Build Self-Improvement and take yourself seriously.

LARRY M. JACKSON

ARIMUS PUBLISHING LLC

i

Published 2021 by Arimus Publishing LLC.

ISBN 978-1-7369578-0-6

Cover Design by Larry M. Jackson
Edited by Malory of The Missing Ink

For permission requests, contact the publisher through the information listed below.

information@larrymjackson.com

ARIMUS PUBLISHING LLC.
952 Golf House Road W
Suite I-608
Whitsett, NC 27377

Ph: (336)223-4824
Fax: (336)449-4231

Arimus Publishing LLC.

For Mom, Lilah, Micah, Landon, Liam, Lathan –

You've always inspired me to never stop trying.

Preface

The Modified Toolbox was created as a way for men to spark internal reflection, self-discovery and inspire a personal journey towards self-development and social accountability. Constructed and presented in an easy to read and easy to digest format, the Toolbox allows a reader to start on any page and begin their journey or spur a topic of discussion within a group setting.

"As men, we have the responsibility to give the world our truest and purest form of integrity...but first, we must give it to ourselves".

- Larry M. Jackson

Becoming a better person doesn't happen overnight. So take your time and build a legacy that will.

⬦ The Modified Gentleman places an emphasis on men becoming the best "version" of themselves. Take your Life's Lessons and use them as fuel to propel yourself forward.

Do not let your negative behaviors become your identity.

✦ At times, a good person can make a bad decision...but that doesn't make them a bad person. It makes them human, and the lesson learned from that choice hits a lot deeper and makes their growth more meaningful.

You are the General in command of your own happiness. Never look for another person to make you happy. Only look for another person that can add to it.

❖ It will be impossible for you to make someone else happy...if you can't make yourself happy to begin with. First learn how to satisfy your own needs before you put forth the time, energy and effort of adding to someone else's happiness.

Shout out to all of the Gentlemen who haven't felt okay lately, but still get up every day and refuse to quit.

Stay Strong!

✧ *It's rough out there for men. It can be extremely exhausting holding your emotions in all the time if that's all you've ever known. A lot of men are going through tough times and they still manage to hold their head up high and push forward when they're not feeling well. Gentleman...check up on each other. Sometimes just asking how a person is doing can make a world of difference.*

No one tells you this
but sometimes the
healing hurts more
than the wound.

The personal journey you embark upon to do
the internal work is extremely important. It is
one of the hardest, toughest and most valuable
adventures you will ever set out to face. You
should also pack a lunch, it may be a long one.
But worth it.

When you're ahead of your time...the hardest part is learning how patience works.

Impatience + Ignorance = Failure

Don't rush the process. Take your time and learn as you grow.

Life doesn't care about who you "want" to be, because it already has plans for who you "need" to be.

◈ Read that again...

Trying to fit in...is a form of suicide.

Being your true, authentic self is also a self-respect multiplier.

Take some time and find your own peace. We've been taught to seek out immediate pleasure and satisfaction whenever we become unsettled.

✦ Women figured it out a long time ago. They're concerned with preserving their peace of mind which in turn leads to their enjoyment of life and results in longer individual satisfaction. On the other hand, men are wired to find immediate pleasure in hopes that it will lead to a moment of peace.

We have to change that.

A broken man can be mended.

His ego can be humbled.

His anger becomes kindness.

His greed turned into charity
and his selfishness into
compassion.

His healing journey now
becomes the map for the next
traveler.

⬦ The only thing permanent in life is death.
As long as there is breath in your lungs, you
can correct your mistakes.

You never completely start over from scratch. Your experience becomes the new starting point.

❖ When you're at an age in life where you have to rebuild...don't panic. Lean on your knowledge and leverage your experience to create a new path leading forward.

Being single while you learn about yourself is greatly underrated. I take myself out on dates. I go out to eat. I go to the park, go fishing, and enjoy a quiet walk. Hop in my truck and go for a nice drive. The peace of just being emotionally self-sustaining is incredible.

💎 *True happiness is in your own hands. It's very important to find it for yourself and not allow anyone else to control it.*

We do not check the refrigerator multiple times to find new food. We check to see if our standards have dropped low enough to eat what is available.

⬦ Men...you can either put in the time, effort and energy to increase the value of your current situation, or you can let your current situation decrease the value in YOU, and what you're worth.

There are only three types of MEN. Those who lower the standard, those who raise the standard, and those who fool themselves into thinking they can do both.

💎 At some point in life, you have to pick a side, and when you do, your level of resolve will let you know if you've made the right decision or not.

The 4 Horsemen of Your Worst-Self

- *laziness*

- *distraction*

- *ignorance*

- *fear*

💎 These 4 aspects of life are extremely powerful.
Just one of them can derail your progress in life.
So how do we defeat them?

DISCIPLINE
---
laziness

💎 *Laziness wants to be your best friend. He'll beg you to hang out with him all day, every day. Tell him you're busy. You have "Life" to do. DISCIPLINE will keep you on track when laziness shows up.*

PRIORITY
---
distraction

✦ *Distraction is the Curator of a million dreams.*
You have to WAKE UP! *Focus your energy on the*
order of importance and PRIORITIZE *the things*
that are most meaningful in your life.

KNOWLEDGE

---

ignorance

Ignorance is a very confident Horseman and
he thinks he knows it all. However, true
KNOWLEDGE allows you to never stop
learning from everyone and everything.

COURAGE

---

fear

✧ *Fear is the strongest Horseman and has incredibly thick skin. We must sharpen our COURAGE to cut through it. Never let your edge become dull or fear will quickly overtake you.*

YOU

PROCRASTINATION

♦ *Plot twist! Procrastination is their King. He commands The 4 Horsemen of your Worst-Self and he leads them into battle against you every day. What is the status of your life at this very moment? It's either because you've beaten Procrastination and his army, or...they've beaten you.*

The uncertainty of life can be scary if that's all you focus on but remember, the caterpillar doesn't know what's on the other side either...it just trusts the process.

❖ Sometimes opportunity knocks...but if you pretend not to be home...it'll just move on down to your neighbor's house.

Sometimes there is "No Support". No friends, no family, no free-ride. Most times...it's just you and the strength of your determination to make a change. Never take it personal, just execute.

💎 A lot of people don't succeed at their goals because they lack a strong internal support in themselves. Yes...you can support yourself, it is perfectly fine. We let external support sources overwhelm our internal...but at some point, those external sources go away, so who do you think is left spending all day, day-dreaming about those goals?

Be your own biggest fan.

Pray that mistake humbles you and not let the achievement gas you up.

Our circumstances can be similar but our reactions are 100% personal. The same boiling water that softens the potato will harden the egg.

Stop focusing on FINDING *the right person. Start focusing on* BECOMING *the right person.*

Build the right standards for yourself and
the right people will find you.

OUTGROW

your own

*bullsh*t.*

💎 *Do I really need to explain this one?*

HAPPINESS
PURPOSE
FULFILLMENT
PEACE
PROGRESS
PASSION
ME
HEALTH
GOALS
STABILITY
POSITIVITY
DISCIPLINE
AMBITION

Surround yourself with positive intention. Think it. Visualize it. Feel it. Speak it. Hear it. Smell it if you have to...just make it happen.

I *know...growth sucks*
but stop trying to cut
corners and dodging it.

Put in the work.

Do it.

Get it done.

The "*future you*" is tired
of waiting.

⬧ Respect the beauty that comes with the struggle.

Less *focus on the possibility.*

More *focus on making it possible.*

✦ *This is an important one for my analytical guys out there. It can be very easy to become a victim of "Paralysis by Analysis". This is where you get stuck in the "planning" phase and never make it to the "action" phase.*

Get started. Be flexible. Learn to adapt as you grow.

Healing is weird. Some days you're okay and you're doing fine. Other days it still hurts like it's fresh. It's a process with no definitive time-frame. You just have to keep going and know that when all is said and done, you're going to be okay.

✦ If you pick at the scab before it is healed...it will start to bleed again. At times, it still itches and demands your focus and attention but you must leave it alone and respect the healing process. It works on its own time-frame, not yours. You can't force yourself to be healed. However, during the healing process is where you focus on not repeating the actions that caused the injury in the first place.

Be *a savage towards your*
Peace, Purpose and
Progress. Be *mean.* Be
rude. Be *heartless and*
brutal. Kill *the noise that*
distracts *you because its*
job *is to stop you.*

◈ Protecting and nurturing your internal growth
and relationship with yourself will be one of the
most important relationships you will ever have.

How do men become better as a whole? Find a proper mentor. If you can't find one...level yourself the f*ck up and become one.

◈ Once you become aware of your potential, the only thing that can stop you, IS YOU!

- 32 -

FEEDBACK
failure

◆ *Pay attention. There is always a lesson to be learned.*

You will never truly value and appreciate peace until you experience the chaos it was born from.

⬦ This is life after the "Warrior's Mentality"...after the battles...after the fighting. At some time in a man's life, he will long for a level of peace that is greater than the level chaos.

If you don't disarm
your triggers, they
will backfire on you
every time.

🔹 Even if you put the safety on...they will
still backfire.

Life is an eternal teacher. If you missed the lesson and failed the test, there will be a mandatory retest, and a constant retest until you pass the class.

The lack of
self-respect shows a
lack of all-respect.

Before respect can be earned, it
must first be learned.

What if I told you that not even death could stop you? Leave your mark on this world and you will live forever.

◈ Never just "do things" for the sake of doing them...find a fulfilling purpose and set meaningful goals for yourself.

Just because you're a handyman with a tool-belt...doesn't mean you need to fix every problem.

⬦ Most handymen I've spoken to are great at fixing things but they hate customer service. Keep that in mind when you find yourself running to fix a broken situation.

If you don't find a way to increase the quality in your way of life...your way of life will decrease the quality in you.

1. Find a Purpose.

2. Find some Self-Clarity.

Let go of:
The Pain.
The Hurt.
The Guilt.

Grab a hold of:
YOUR PEACE
YOUR PURPOSE
YOUR PROGRESS

Just focus on
refining your vibe
and I promise, the
Universe will
handle the rest.

💎 *Just be yourself. Let yourself grow, fail,
succeed, laugh, cry, agree, disagree, smile, frown,
love, hate, fight, submit, push, and pull.*

Never let your past, forge weapons that attack your future.

❖ I know...it's easier said than done. Sometimes you don't even know you're forging weapons that will attack you in the future. Stay focused. Pick a positive path and don't forget to forge a strong shield to protect yourself as well.

If it's important enough, nothing can stop you. Not even your own damn self.

✦ Self-sabotage is a dirty trickster and he's extremely good at his job.

How your life feels
on the inside is more
important than how
it looks on the
outside.

PROOF

---

promises

💎 *The proof of your character will validate
the worth of your promises.*

Expect nothing...but appreciate everything.

Being thankful is a
two-way street.
Make sure you look
both ways before
crossing.

*Being able to send and receive gratitude is
a skill of genuine integrity.*

Imagine being super excited about an idea, then being even more afraid of it failing...or it actually working.

What do you do when both failure
and success scares you at the same time?
Simple...you just TRY.

The only rule to being yourself...is to never stop being yourself.

❖ Remember what I said earlier
about trying to fit in?

Stop telling yourself that you're going to start over. Instead, tell yourself you're going to try again and do it differently this time.

All you need to do is START and KEEP GOING. You will end up exactly where you need to be.

✧ When it comes to our own story, we know the beginning and we know the ending we want. It's the details in the middle that we need to sort out.

Get Healthy.

Get Educated.

Get Money.

Get Spiritual.

Get Organized.

Build Your Legacy.

You're growth, progress and success are 100% your responsibility. No one is going to do it for you.

STOP!!
I *don't know who needs to hear this, but* STOP!
STOP *pretending you're okay!*
STOP *pretending you aren't hurting!*
STOP *pretending there isn't pain!*
STOP *pretending everything is fine!*
STOP *pretending you have it all put together and* START...*being real with yourself.*

Everyone has a sad story. You can either turn yours into an anchor or a rocket ship. Choose wisely.

💎 One can hold you back and one can take you to places you've never seen.

Too many people spend their time looking fly but never actually get off the ground.

💎 *The focus is to become so fulfilled with living your life that you never noticed how high in the clouds you are...until someone tells you.*

Stop caging your emotions and let them run free. You'll be surprised where they lead you.

Being a "People Pleaser" is not a valid job title.

💎 Trust me...it's a saturated market.

Stop giving away your power.

What makes you strong is your unique strength. What weakens you is when you give that strength away without properly recharging yourself. The hard part is that it usually takes something as equally unique to recharge you.

As *men*, we are logical and external. We connect upfront and face to face with the world. However, the world may not connect with us because we're afraid to let it in. We have to internally change our mindset so we can fully experience what the world has to offer.

LIMIT.

THEIR.

ACCESS.

❖ Setting boundaries for yourself and how people
approach you is a form of positive self-control.
Always remember, "If you let them...they will."

Unlearning something harmful is just as important as learning something beneficial.

💎 When you expand your focus, your field of view also changes.

Focus so strongly on your personal growth that you'll be able to say "NO" without fear and "YES" with full courage.

✵ Once you've found peace and settled your "Internal World"...the external world won't be able to shake you.

Nothing beats good old-fashioned, homegrown, self-sustaining happiness.

✧ It *doesn't matter if you're married or single,*
developing a better understanding of yourself is
something that can never be taken away from you.

Stop playing around and take yourself seriously.

⬦ The secret is reading between the lines.

These words promote a sense of self-awareness that will lead you to Accountability, Responsibility, Planning, Learning, Healing, Growing, Forgiving, Self-Development, Improvement, Fulfillment, Happiness, Peace, Purpose, and ultimate Positive Progression with Understanding.

Listen...if you don't take yourself seriously...why would you expect anyone else to?

"There are only two times in a man's life when he is truly invincible. When he has nothing to lose and when he has everything to lose."

- The Modified Gentleman -

◈ This is where a man starts to truly find himself. This is where his METTLE is tested. This is where he truly finds what his core is made of. How does he react when he has everything? How does he react when he has nothing? You're going to travel this road your entire life but the rewards you pick up along the way will last forever.

It's a new day. You've got this!

❖ Remember...always hold your head high as you go out and face the day!

About the Author

Larry M. Jackson is a passionate advocate for men's mental health and wellness. He grew up in Florence, SC in a single-parent home where his mother placed a strong emphasis on values and self-respect. As a young man struggling to find his way in life, he noticed the lack of positive male mentorship and not only how it affected his life and his community, but how it affected young men in general.

His passion to help others lead him to become a Certified Life Coach in addition to creating The Modified Gentleman, an organization aimed at helping men manage depression, stress and trauma while finding the meaning within their lives. He has attained multiple college degrees and is also a 10 year veteran of the United States Army.

"I strongly believe that positive male mentorship can make a huge difference in a young man's life but we must first learn to mentor ourselves." - Larry M. Jackson

Acknowledgements:

- Linda - Glenda - Josey - Charlotte - Lorrie -

- Travis - Pierre - Kevin - Dewayne - Reggie - Cliff - Darrell

- Ahmad - Dietrich - Gary - Eric - Brian - James

- And to all of the dads, husbands, sons, grandfathers, brothers, uncles, cousins, friends, positive role-models, mentors and gentlemen out there doing their best to navigate this world.

Each day is a test of your strength. Find Peace. Find Purpose. Stay Strong and NEVER give up.

If you ever feel that you can't go on any further, please contact the National Suicide Prevention Lifeline at 1-800-273-8255 or visit www.suicidepreventionlifeline.org for more information. This telephone number will also service veterans.

More on the book, please visit www.themodifiedtoolbox.com

For more on The Modified Gentleman, you can find us at:

www.themodifiedgentleman.com

YouTube: The Modified Gentleman Channel

Instagram: @themodifiedgentleman